A
MEDIEVAL
MONASTERY

Series Editor	David Salariya
Book Editor	Jenny Millington
Consultant	Glyn Coppack

Author:
Fiona Macdonald studied history at Cambridge University and at the University of East Anglia. She has taught children, adults and undergraduates. She has written many books on historical topics, mainly for children.

Illustrator:
Gerald Wood was born in London and began his career in film advertising. He then illustrated magazines for many years before becoming a book illustrator specialising in historical reconstruction.

Consultant:
Glyn Coppack is an acknowledged authority on monastic archaeology and has directed many major research excavations. He is currently Head of Historic Branch and Historic Properties for the Midland and East Anglia region of English Heritage. He is also a fellow of the Society of Antiquaries of London.

Created, designed and produced by
The Salariya Book Co Ltd, Brighton, UK

First published in paperback 1996
by Macdonald Young Books Ltd

First published in hardback in 1994
by Simon & Schuster Young Books

Macdonald Young Books Ltd
Campus 400
Maylands Avenue
Hemel Hempstead
Herts
HP2 7EZ

0 7500 2045 8

A catalogue record for this book is available from the British Library.

Printed and bound in Hong Kong by Wing King Tong

A MEDIEVAL MONASTERY

FIONA MACDONALD   GERALD WOOD

MACDONALD YOUNG BOOKS

CONTENTS

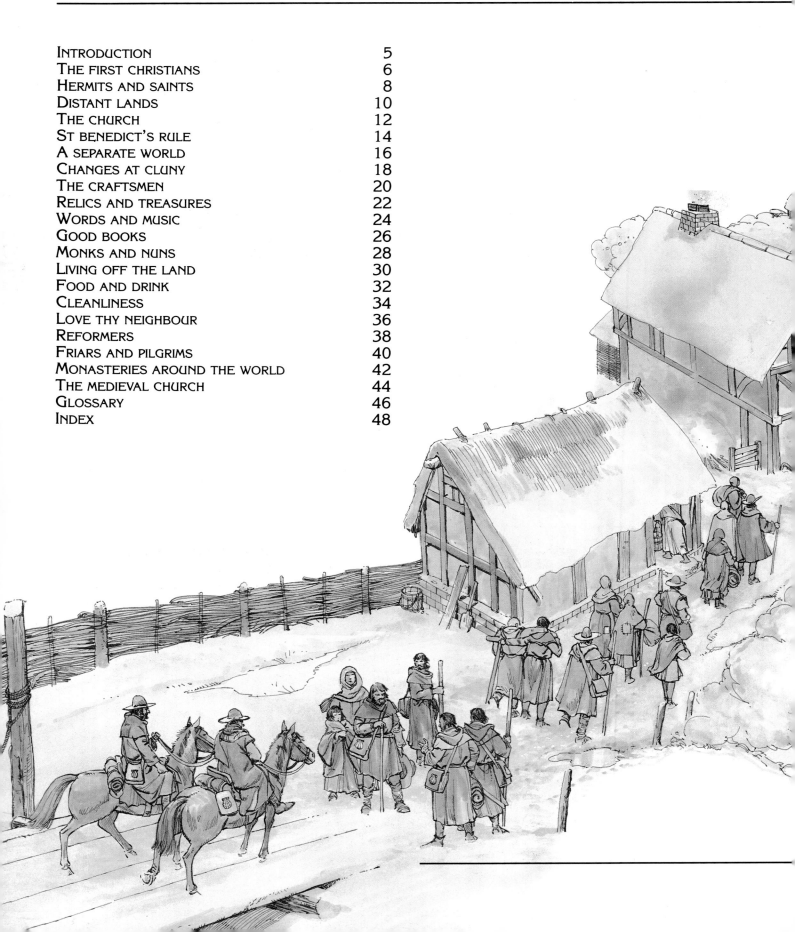

INTRODUCTION

In the early Middle Ages (around AD 400-1000), some Christian men and women left their families and friends to live a disciplined and lonely life. They had no money, no possessions and no freedom. They wore rough clothes and ate little food. Why did they choose to shut themselves away in monasteries (for men) or nunneries (for women) 'like sheep in a sheepfold', as one medieval poet said?

A monk or nun would have found that question easy to answer: monasteries (and nunneries) were 'powerhouses of prayer'. Prayer was a way of talking to God, and monks and nuns devoted a large part of their time to it. They hoped to win blessings for themselves and for the rest of society, and

they asked God not to punish people for their sins in the life after death.

Soon, monks and nuns began to take on many other tasks. They ran schools, wrote books, set up hospitals and helped the poor. They provided retirement homes for elderly men and women, and a safe place to send young daughters to school. Leading monks and nuns sometimes became politicians.

After around AD 1200, many monasteries declined. Monks and nuns became lazy, and skimped their work and prayers. New religious groups grew up to replace the old ones, winning greater respect. But some monks and nuns kept faith with monasteries' original aims, and continued to serve God and other people all their lives.

THE FIRST CHRISTIANS

The medieval monks and nuns you can read about in this book were all inspired by the teachings of Jesus of Nazareth, who was the founder of Christianity. He was executed by the Roman Governor of Judea (present-day Israel, Jordan and Palestine) as a trouble-maker in AD 33. But he was also a preacher and a prophet. There had been other Jewish prophets before him, but none had so great an impact worldwide.

Jesus's message was a challenge to Roman rule, which was hated by many con-quered nations. Jesus's followers – wherever they lived – believed he had called them to live a new sort of life; they felt they should form Christian communities, helping one another and worshipping God.

In the years after Jesus's execution, the number of people following his teaching grew rapidly. The map on these pages shows how far the Christian faith had spread by AD 600. In spite of persecutions, the first Christians shared a life of prayer and worship, and established a yearly pattern of fasting and festivals based on earlier, pagan rituals that were mostly connected with the farming year. Many of these survived throughout the Middle Ages, and are still celebrated today.

IRELAND

ENGLAND

GERMANY

FRANCE

KEY

Areas converted to Christianity by AD 600.

SPAIN

NORTH AFRICA

THE CHRISTIAN YEAR

Easter (March/April) celebrates Jesus appearing to his friends after he had been crucified.

Whitsun (May/June) commemorates God sending his Holy Spirit (often pictured as a dove) to guide Christians.

Michelmas (September) is a harvest-time festival, in honour of the archangel Michael; a time of thanksgiving.

Halloween (October) – All Souls' Eve, when the dead are remembered and prayed for. Ghosts are believed to appear.

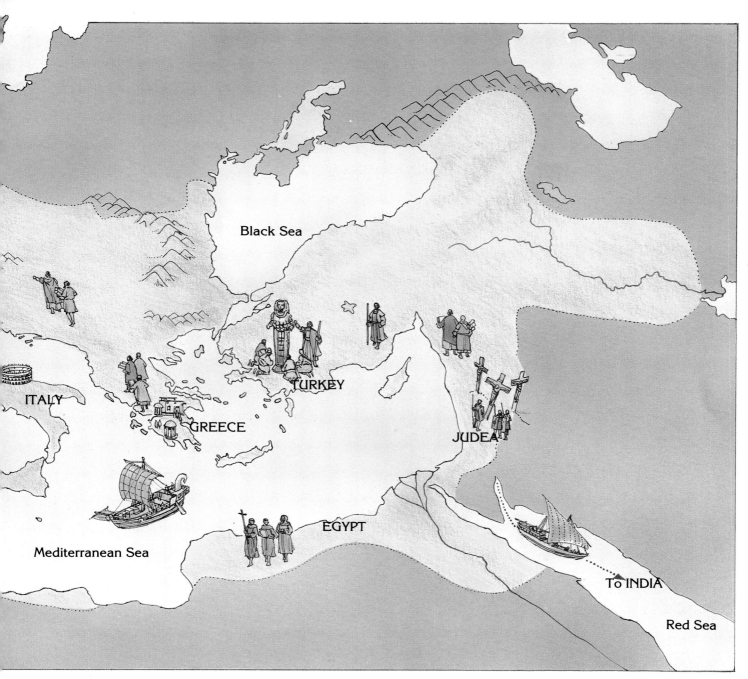

Black Sea

TURKEY

ITALY

GREECE

JUDEA

EGYPT

Mediterranean Sea

To INDIA

Red Sea

Advent (November/ December) the 4 weeks before Christmas, when Christians look forward to the birth of Jesus.

Christmas (December) is the festival celebrating the day Jesus was born in a stable in the town of Bethlehem.

Annunciation (March) is the time when, Christians believe, an angel told the Virgin Mary she would give birth to God's son.

Lent (February/March) – 40 days before Easter, when Christians remember Jesus's suffering and death.

HERMITS AND SAINTS

'Behold, how good and pleasant it is for brothers to live together...' These words, from the ancient Book of Psalms (part of the Bible) were often quoted during the Middle Ages. Medieval monks thought this proved that their monastic lifestyle – living together in big religious communities – had been ordered by God. But in fact, the very first monks and nuns lived in a completely different way. They were hermits, seeking solitary refuge in the empty countryside.

Like other early Christians, these hermit monks and nuns believed that civilisation was corrupt; people only seemed to care about

St Antony (?251-356) was one of the earliest hermits, or 'desert fathers'.

St Mary of Egypt (5th century, below) prayed in the desert for so long that her clothes fell to bits.

St Francis of Assisi (1181-1226) loved all creatures, and preached God's message to them.

St Nicholas (d. before 399, below) was a bishop. Legends tell how he brought back to life three children who had been cut up and pickled.

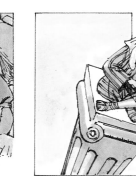

St Jerome (c.331-420) was a scholar, who lived in a cave. Legends say that he was kept company by a lion.

St Symeon Stylites (d. 459) lived at the top of a pillar for 37 years, offering prayers and good advice to onlookers.

This picture (below) from a 14th century manuscript, shows the relics of St Alban being carried in procession.

The remains (or 'relics') of dead saints were treasured by later Christians, who believed they worked miracles.

making money. The Christian hermits thought this neglect of spiritual values, such as honesty, loyalty and charity, was disastrous for individuals and for society as a whole. So they chose to become outcasts, preferring (as they said) 'to store up treasure in heaven' by living pure, holy, simple lives, far away from everyone else.

Gradually, this hermit lifestyle changed. Groups of men and women decided to live together in communities, called monasteries and nunneries, which they dedicated to God. It was safer, and they could share routine tasks. But these early monks and nuns still lived rather like hermits. They each had individual cells, and spent their days in private prayer.

St Catherine's monastery (above), in the Sinai desert (between Israel and Egypt), was founded in the 6th century. Many early monks travelled to desert lands in search of solitude. The monastery buildings were surrounded by a strong wall, to protect the monks from robbers and wild animals.

The monastery of Mount Athos, in Greece (top), founded in 936. Monks came here to live as hermits, and to build new religious communities. Women – and female animals – were not allowed to set foot on this holy ground.

Right
Remote monasteries, like this one in the Alps between France and Italy, helped monks to feel close to God.

DISTANT LANDS

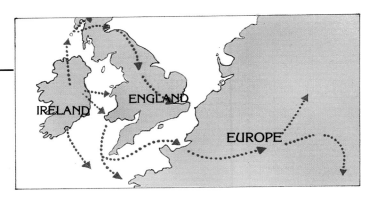

The first monasteries were built in the Middle East. But before long, eager missionaries carried news of the Christian faith to the far corners of Europe, and to China and India as well.

Nobody knows when the first Christians reached Ireland, but archaeologists have found the remains of early churches dating from c.500. A 10th-century poem tells how one monk hoped to live: 'I wish for a secret hut in the wilderness . . . It should face south, for warmth . . . I would like a few wise companions, to pray with me, and a lovely church, with fine linen, candles and a copy of the Bible . . . We would grow leeks and raise chickens . . . and pray to God in every place.'

Not all Irish monks stayed peacefully at home. Irish missionaries travelled to Scotland, Italy, Switzerland, France and the north of England, spreading their faith. In this Christian 'frontier territory', they chose well-defended sites for monasteries, such as Mont St Michel in France, and Lindisfarne island and Whitby on the north-eastern coast of England.

Missionary monks travelled across Europe (above) to spread the Christian faith.

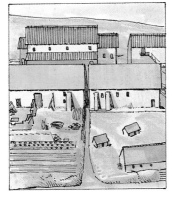

St Columba founded the monastery at Iona (above) in 563. The first kings of Scotland were buried here.

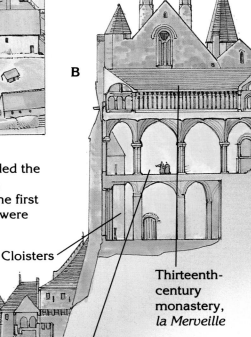

B

Cloisters

Scriptorium

Thirteenth-century monastery, *la Merveille*

The 13th-century monastery known as *la Merveille* was built in the Gothic style. The scriptorium, on the second floor, was the place where the monks copied and illuminated books for the monastery library.

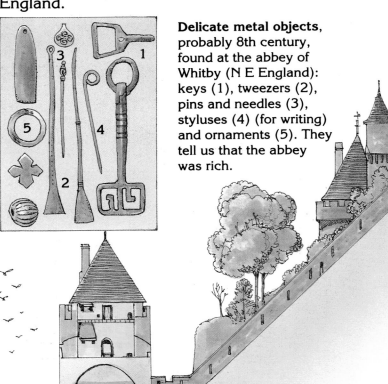

Delicate metal objects, probably 8th century, found at the abbey of Whitby (N E England): keys (1), tweezers (2), pins and needles (3), styluses (4) (for writing) and ornaments (5). They tell us that the abbey was rich.

A

Monks' church, Iona (above). Bible stories (below) were carved on crosses outside Irish monasteries.

Two monasteries (above) were built at Mont St Michel. The first was 7th-century, rebuilt around 1000. The second was founded in the 13th century.

Mont Saint Michel, in Brittany, France, was founded in 966. Because of its dramatic site on a rocky island, it was called a 'monastic fortress'. It could be reached on foot only at low tide. For the rest of the time, the monks were safely surrounded by sea. Sites like this were favoured by Celtic monks. The 7th century monastery at Lindisfarne, off the Northumbrian coast, was also built on an island.

The cloisters (right) at Mont St Michel, where monks could walk and talk.

The monks' church (A) and the monastery buildings (B) are perched on rocky ledges around the slopes of the island. The church foundations are 73.6 metres above sea-level.

THE CHURCH

At first, Christianity was not a well-organised religion. Local Christian communities – including monasteries – chose leaders from among themselves, then waited for guidance from the 'apostles'. These were Jesus's friends and disciples. After his death, they devoted their lives to travelling through the Mediterranean lands, preaching and teaching.

As more and more people became Christians, these simple arrangements were not enough. Without a central authority to say what the Christian faith was and how Christians should worship, mistakes could be made. So an elaborate organisation grew up, headed by the Pope (Bishop of Rome). He was successor to the apostle St Peter, who had set up the first Christian community there. Later, many new Church jobs were created, each with its own responsibilities.

The Pope was head of the Church. In the Middle Ages, he was spiritual leader of all Christian men and women in Western Europe. Popes gave guidance on all religious issues; they also played an important part in medieval politics.

Pope

Novice

The hierarchy – power structure – of the Catholic Church (below). Archbishops and bishops were responsible for administering dioceses (large areas). Priests and deacons (trainee priests) cared for people living in smaller areas, called parishes. Monks and nuns lived in separate communities, ruled by an abbot or an abbess; some monks were also priests. Friars were priests who travelled around the countryside preaching and teaching.

Archbishop   Bishop   Priest   Deacon   Monk   Abbess   Nun   Friars

Rich parents decide their second son will be a monk; the oldest will inherit the family's lands.

At home, the boy is taught some Latin by the family's chaplain, who is a priest.

Aged about 8, the boy is taken to the monastery. It will be his home for the rest of his life.

He goes to classes at the monastery school, and is trained as a monk by the novice-master.

He learns about the Christian faith, and how to take part in services in the monks' church.

He makes his first vows, and also receives the 'tonsure', a special haircut.

After several years as a novice, he makes his final vows of poverty, chastity and obedience.

Now he is a full member of the holy community. Young girls were trained by nuns in the same way.

As the rest of Church became more organised, there were attempts to organise monasteries and nunneries, as well. It was almost impossible to control isolated hermits, but, where men or women lived in communities, strict rules – for example, about daily routine, or training to become a monk – could be made. Around 520, an Italian, St Benedict of Nursia, drew up detailed rules for monks (see page 14).

Knight templar

Right
Parents gave very young children to monasteries, along with money, hoping the child's prayers would help their family's future. By the 12th century, religious leaders condemned this cruel practice.

Knights templar (left) were monks who fought in the crusades.

St Benedict's Rule

Midnight Monks are woken for the first church service of the day, called Matins ('morning').

1.00 am Monks remain in church for the second service of the day, called Lauds ('praise').

2.00 am Monks leave church and go back to bed. They can sleep, or read holy books, or pray.

7.00 am Monks are woken, and return to church for a short service called 'Prime' ('first').

For over 500 years, St Benedict's rule governed the lives of monks and nuns in many parts of Europe. They even came to be known as 'Benedictines', after him. What did St Benedict hope his rule would achieve?

In his own words, he explained it like this: 'I have written this Rule, so that by following it in our monasteries, we monks may show that we have some goodness in our lives, and the beginnings of holiness'. He also wanted to make sure that monks and nuns spent their days in the best possible way, and did not become lazy, wicked or bored.

But what was the best way for monks and nuns to live? For Benedict, there were two simple answers to that question: 'do God's work' and 'keep busy'. By 'God's work', he meant prayer and worship. Quoting a text from the Bible ('Seven times have I prayed to Thee, O Lord'), he ordered monks to attend church services seven times a day. When they were not in church, St Benedict wanted monks to do hard physical work, such as farming, or, if they were well-educated, to study and make copies of important religious books.

Benedict also said that monks should never leave their monasteries. They should have no possessions, and they should be generous, charitable, clean, pure and obedient. Often, these new rules were ignored, but at least they set a very high standard to aim for.

8.30 am To church for a second Mass, then to the Chapter House to hear notices and discuss plans.

9.30 am After the Chapter meeting, junior monks were free to walk and talk in the cloisters.

11.30 am If monks were old or weak, they were allowed to rest now for an hour.

7.30 am After Prime, some monks remain in the church to celebrate the first Mass of the day.

Mass was the Church's most important service; monks, servants and farmhands could attend.

7.30 am Monks not attending Mass washed and (once a week) changed their clothes.

8.00 am Breakfast time. On fast days, monks were meant to go without breakfast.

10.00 am Back to church for High Mass, the most solemn service, with hymns and chanting.

10.30 am Senior monks organise the servants and labourers on the monks' farms.

Some monks worked long hours on the farms themselves; others did only a little hard labour.

11.00 am Dinner. Monks listened to readings from holy books. Talking was not allowed.

12.30 to 5 pm (left) Monks worked in the fields, or in herb gardens.

5.00 pm (6.00 pm in summer) (right). To church for service of Vespers ('evening') and Collation (holy readings).

6.00 pm (7.00 pm in summer). After supper, monks could relax in the cloisters or the gardens.

If it was cold, monks would gather in the warming room, the only room with heating.

7.00 pm (8.00 pm in summer) Service called Compline ('ending'), then monks went to bed.

A SEPARATE WORLD

Because Benedictine monks and nuns were not meant to leave their monasteries, St Benedict declared that their monasteries must, therefore, contain everything they needed to live a good, religious life. There must be a church, of course, but also many other types of building, to cater for the monks' or nuns' well-being. They needed somewhere to sleep, somewhere to wash, a place to eat, a place to read and write, somewhere to take exercise, and a hospital in case they fell ill.

The abbot or abbess – the leader of the community – needed separate living quarters, with rooms to receive guests travelling on Church business. Monks or nuns needed a garden to grow herbs to make medicines. There were also stables, storerooms, rooms for servants, lavatories, and a gatehouse. This guarded the entrance to the monastery, but was also the place where poor people might come to beg for food and clothes.

Over the years, monasteries that followed the rule of St Benedict grew larger and more prosperous, as they were given land, money and goods by wealthy people hoping to win forgiveness from God with their generous gifts. The largest of them, for example the monastery of Cluny in eastern France (founded in 910), were like separate little worlds. By the 12th century, there were almost 500 monks living at Cluny, and probably an equal number of lay-brothers (helpers) and servants. This made it bigger than many villages of the time.

The isolation could often help the monks find peace and quiet to concentrate on God. But some people said they were remote and over-protected from the risks and troubles of everyday life.

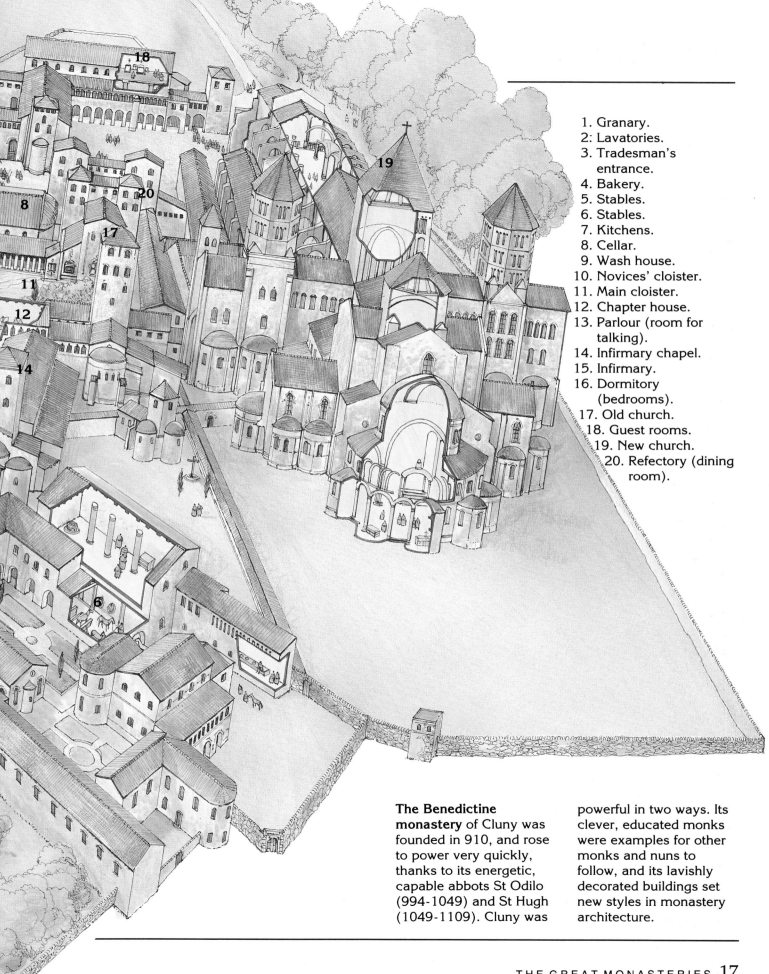

1. Granary.
2. Lavatories.
3. Tradesman's entrance.
4. Bakery.
5. Stables.
6. Stables.
7. Kitchens.
8. Cellar.
9. Wash house.
10. Novices' cloister.
11. Main cloister.
12. Chapter house.
13. Parlour (room for talking).
14. Infirmary chapel.
15. Infirmary.
16. Dormitory (bedrooms).
17. Old church.
18. Guest rooms.
19. New church.
20. Refectory (dining room).

The Benedictine monastery of Cluny was founded in 910, and rose to power very quickly, thanks to its energetic, capable abbots St Odilo (994-1049) and St Hugh (1049-1109). Cluny was powerful in two ways. Its clever, educated monks were examples for other monks and nuns to follow, and its lavishly decorated buildings set new styles in monastery architecture.

CHANGES AT CLUNY

In the 9th century, a monk called Benedict of Aniane wrote a revised version of St Benedict's rule, bringing it up to date. In later years, other monks introduced far more substantial changes to the monastic routine, though they claimed still to be inspired by St Benedict's ideas. At Cluny, for example, monks did very little work, but spent most of their time in church. They wrote and performed beautiful hymns and services. Their aim, they assured people, was to give glory to God, not to take pride and pleasure in their own skills.

This cultured, artistic lifestyle suited the Cluny monks very well. They came mostly from noble families, and were not used to working on the land. Outsiders – and some churchmen – complained about this, but the fiercest criticism came when, led by Abbot Hugh, they commissioned a magnificent new church. They wanted this vast building (over 100 metres long) to be as impressive and elaborate as their singing, so they decorated it with wall paintings, carvings and statues.

St Hugh planned a magnificent new church for the abbey of Cluny. Work began in 1088, and continued until 1157. St Hugh hoped to turn the monastery into a 'new Jerusalem' – a heavenly city here on earth. He was also inspired by a dream which Gunzo, one of the Cluny monks, reported to him. Gunzo said that St Peter had appeared in his dream, and ordered him to tell Hugh to build a mighty church. Cluny's new church was dedicated (offered to God at a special service) by Pope Urban II in 1095. A rival monk, St Bernard of Clairvaux, said: 'Oh vanity of vanities – and foolish, too. The walls are splendid, but the poor are not there.'

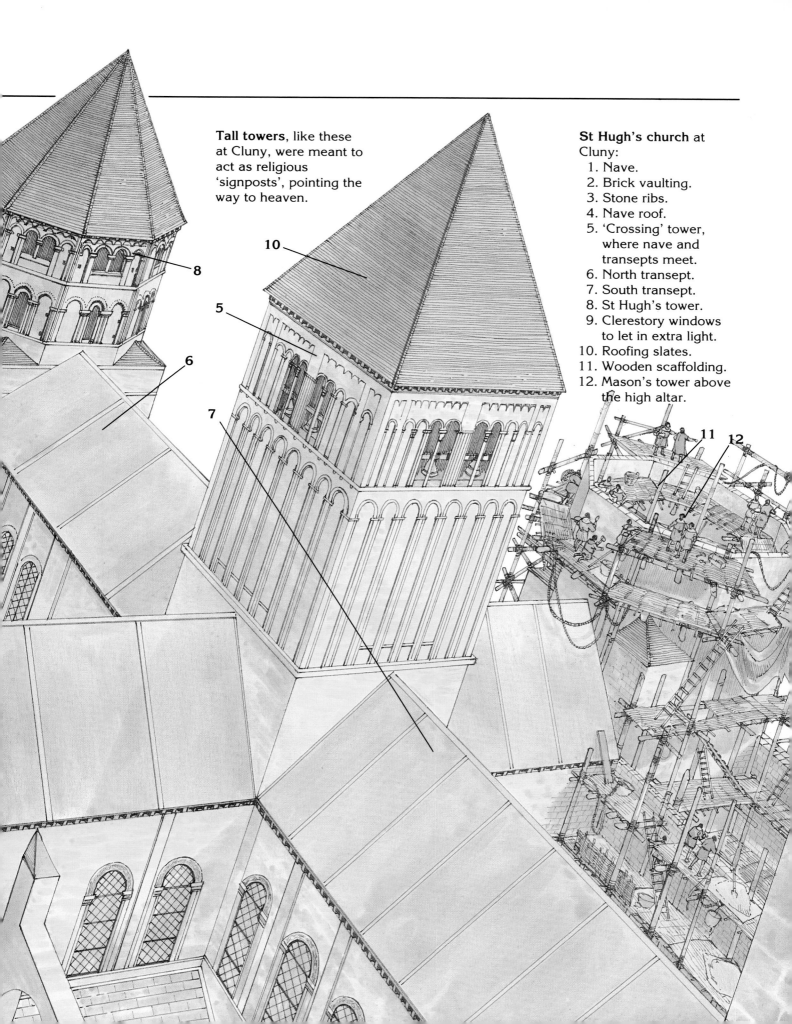

Tall towers, like these at Cluny, were meant to act as religious 'signposts', pointing the way to heaven.

St Hugh's church at Cluny:
1. Nave.
2. Brick vaulting.
3. Stone ribs.
4. Nave roof.
5. 'Crossing' tower, where nave and transepts meet.
6. North transept.
7. South transept.
8. St Hugh's tower.
9. Clerestory windows to let in extra light.
10. Roofing slates.
11. Wooden scaffolding.
12. Mason's tower above the high altar.

THE CRAFTSMEN

Noble men and women gave large sums of money to help build monasteries. Architects and skilled master masons were employed to produce a building that would look beautiful for God.

Walls were built of expensive stone, cut carefully to shape and winched into position.

The first monks built their one-room shelters with their own hands. They used cheap local materials – rough stone or sun-dried bricks in the desert; timber with turf roofing in Ireland – and simple building techniques.

By the 10th century, things had changed. The great monastic churches, like Cluny, were built by specialist craftsmen, trained in a variety of building skills. These workers were used to producing top quality work for kings and nobles. They knew the monks expected the same high standards. So they used costly materials and time-consuming, expensive techniques. Blocks of stone were shaped to build vaulted ceilings, tall arches and fancy pillars. Windows were decorated with stone

Mortar was mixed from lime (made by burning lumps of chalk or limestone), sand and water. It was important to get the mixture just right. If it was too wet, the walls would fall down.

Carpenters made strong wooden frameworks to support tall arches while they were being built.

They also made thick rafters, to support heavy roofs of slate, lead or clay tiles.

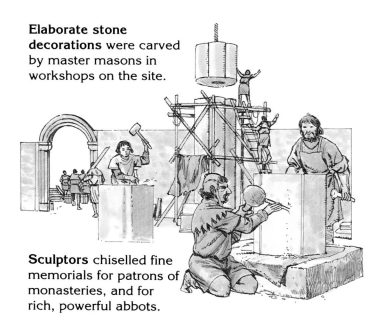

Elaborate stone decorations were carved by master masons in workshops on the site.

Sculptors chiselled fine memorials for patrons of monasteries, and for rich, powerful abbots.

tracery and glazed with hand-made glass. Floors were covered with ceramic tiles.

Even the monks' living quarters were elaborately decorated. At Cluny, for example, and at Norwich, the cloisters, where the monks walked, wrote and studied, were carved with innumerable lively figures. Some showed devils or monsters, others were cartoon-style scenes of everyday life. Most monks were amused and delighted, but St Bernard hated this, too: 'There are so many strange and wonderful shapes to see, that it is more interesting for the monks to read the stonework than a book, and to spend their time admiring these marvels than in thinking about God.'

Carpenters carved wood into elaborate 'thrones' for abbots, and chairs for visitors to use.

They also made the choir-stalls (benches) where the monks stood during services.

Blacksmiths made locks for doors and treasure-chests, bars for windows, and chains to secure books.

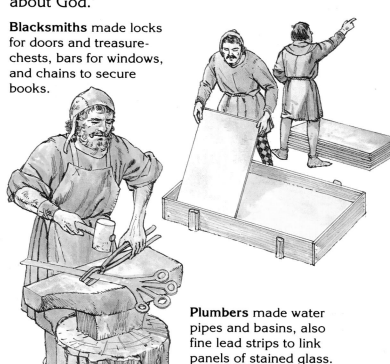

Plumbers made water pipes and basins, also fine lead strips to link panels of stained glass.

RELICS AND TREASURES

Many medieval monasteries wanted fine buildings, and collected rare and beautiful treasures. Many exquisite works of art, made of gold, silver, and precious stones, have survived until today. According to the monks, these treasures helped people to think about God; they also revealed the wealth and high status of the monastery that owned them.

Many monasteries collected the relics (remains) of saints, which were displayed in special shrines. Relics made the monks feel safe; they hoped 'their' dead saint would watch over them from heaven, and protect them. Relics attracted pilgrims to the monastery church; they paid to see (or even touch) the saint's remains, and for the monks to say special prayers. In this way, relics became a useful source of income for the monastic community.

But even the most popular set of relics could not earn enough to pay for wonderful new buildings, or for crosses and candlesticks decorated with gold. So where did the money come from? Partly, from monasteries' own estates. Monks (or their servants) farmed land they had been given, and sold the crops. Extra money came from wealthy men and women, in return for the monks' prayers after they were dead.

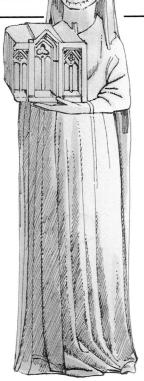

Jeanne of Evreux (above), a French noblewoman, with a model of the chapel she gave money to build.

Relics (the hand-bones) of St Attala (right), abbess of St Stephen's nunnery in Strasbourg (France), carefully preserved in a beautiful container made of crystal and silver-gilt.

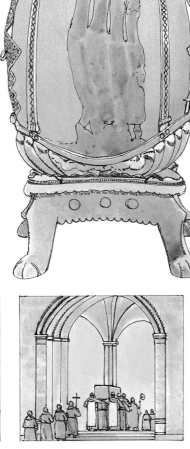

THE STORY OF ST CUTHBERT

Cuthbert was Abbot of Lindisfarne, a monastery on an island. He died in 687.

Cuthbert was a holy man. In 698, the monks said he was a saint. They put his body in a splendid shrine.

In 875, Vikings attacked Lindisfarne. The monks escaped, taking St Cuthbert's body with them.

In 995, Vikings attacked again. The monks built a new shrine for St Cuthbert in Durham.

Gilding a metal cross:
1. Clean off any grease.
2. Coat with gold and mercury.
3. Heat cross, so that mercury evaporates.
4. Polish with a file.

Making a bronze statue:
5. Make a wax model.
6. Surround wax model with clay. Heat clay; wax will melt.
7. Fill space inside block with molten bronze. Leave to cool.
8. Break clay to reveal new bronze statue.

Making a statue base:
9. Carve a wooden mould. Beat sheet-metal into shape.
10. Scratch patterns on the metal.
11. Decorate with figures, using a sharp tool.

The lid of St Cuthbert's coffin (below).

Container (above) for relics ('reliquary') of crystal and gold enamel. Made in Germany in 1200.

Pilgrims crawl into a shrine to touch the relics of a saint.

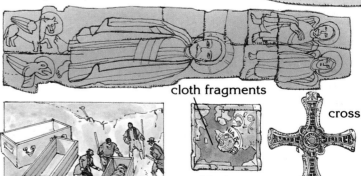

cloth fragments

cross

comb   altar

Throughout the Middle Ages, pilgrims came to pray at St Cuthbert's shrine, hoping for help.

In 1539, King Henry VIII gave orders to destroy St Cuthbert's shrine, and the monastery nearby.

But, inside the shrine, St Cuthbert's coffin was safe. Archaeologists opened it in 1827.

They found his skeleton, a cross, a comb, a portable altar and the remains of rich robes.

WORDS AND MUSIC

Nuns in church. Left to right: sacristan ringing bells, cellarer, abbess, nuns singing, priest, clerk with book, candle-bearers, clerk with cross, clerks with incense, priest at altar.

Music played an important part in the life of the medieval church. The words of many services were chanted, not spoken. This music was called 'plainsong', and it could be sung by all the monks or nuns together, or by different groups taking turns, each one echoing the others. Singing or listening to music like this could generate a dreamy, drifting mood, where it was easy to feel far away from this world, and close to God.

Monks and nuns who were not musically talented could also contribute. They could compose new hymns for chanting, or, like Hrostwitha, a 10th century German nun, write plays to be performed on festival days. Her favourite themes included the lives of saints and martyrs, and featured many heroines.

The Middle Ages is often called an 'age of faith'. That is not entirely true – some medieval people knew little about the Christian message, and cared less. But many people did have genuine beliefs, and the words of surviving medieval hymns can help us understand them. This verse, written by a 12th-century Cluniac monk, reveals widely-held views: 'Brief life is all we have here; Brief sorrow, and brief care; Eternal life without ending; In heaven awaits us there.'

Monks performed plays based on Bible stories on holy days throughout the Christian year. These plays are the origins of present-day theatre.

Bells (above) made of bronze or iron called monks and villagers to prayer. This 11th-century belfry is in Caderousse, southern France.

The earliest surviving English song music (above), written around 1225 at Reading Abbey.

Nuns singing in church (below). Many monks and nuns were trained to read music, and wrote hymns.

A picture from a medieval manuscript (above) shows a row of skulls placed overhead in the choir-stalls, to remind monks that one day they will die.

An owl teaching small birds to read (above). Below, a monk beats a lazy young pupil.

Knight in armour (below), fighting a griffon, a cruel monster rather like a dragon.

Woman chasing a fox away from her geese (below). These four misericords come from Norwich Cathedral.

Right **Decorated misericords** (take-pity seats), which are folded down to let singers rest during long services in church.

'A monastery without books is like a fortress without food.' That's what people said in the Middle Ages. Books stored facts and opinions gathered by earlier generations, keeping them safe for future use. Thanks to copies preserved in monastic libraries, many works by ancient Greek and Roman authors still survive today. Monks and nuns also wrote books themselves; most medieval authors were connected with the Church. There were schools in many communities, where novice monks and nuns, and children of wealthy nobles, were (usually) very well taught.

Medieval books were made of parchment, and the words (in Latin) were hand-written with a quill pen, dipped in thick black ink. Often they were illustrated – or 'illuminated' – with beautiful patterns and pictures.

Above right:

1. Oak cupboard bound with iron, for storing manuscripts at Chester Cathedral, 13th century.

2. Stamp for decorating leather book-bindings.
3. Quill pens, made from goose-feathers.

4. Wooden 'writing-table', coated with wax on the other side, used with:
5. Stylus for making notes.

6. Ivory case, for holding quill pens and, perhaps, knives to scratch errors off the page.

HOW TO MAKE PARCHMENT

Buy a sheepskin or a goatskin. Skins from healthy animals are best. They won't have scars.

Soak in a bath of strong alkali (such as stale urine) to soften and weaken the hairs.

Scrape the hairs off by squeezing the skin between a wooden stick and a wooden beam.

Stretch the skin tightly across a wooden frame, using strong twine made from hemp.

Scrape the skin carefully, to remove any fat or flesh still sticking to it.

Cover the skin with a thick coat of paste, to create a smooth surface for writing. Leave to dry.

Cut strips of parchment from the skin, about 50 cm wide. Trim to give an even thickness.

The finished parchment can now be rolled up, ready to write on with ink made of iron and gall.

Some nuns were allowed to have private rooms (left) as studies, like this one, depicted in a 16th century book.

A page from a famous manuscript, the Grimbald Gospels (below), written and illustrated by English monks in the early 11th century.

A 15th-century chained library. Books were valuable; most used precious inks, golf leaf, and often over 100 sheepskins.

In some monasteries, monks wrote or studied all afternoon. Cubicles like these (called 'carrels') were built for them in the cloisters.

Some monasteries had book-production workshops, where monks worked long hours, making copies of important texts. They wrote astonishingly quickly. In 823 one monk left a note at the end of a book, stating proudly that he had copied all 218 pages in only 7 days. Not all monks felt so satisfied. Other notes have been found, complaining: 'This page is very rough'; 'I am tired'; 'I don't feel well.'

The Abbess was head of the nunnery. She was meant to protect, teach and discipline the nuns.

The Prioress was deputy abbess. Some small nunneries were ruled by a prioress alone.

The **Precentor** was

The Sacristan cared for the holiest part of the

MONKS AND NUNS

Running a large monastery was not an easy task. There were all kinds of jobs to be done – from maintaining calm and discipline to making sure the abbot's horses were fed. Because most monasteries were built in the countryside, there were no shops to buy necessities, and few neighbours to help.

A large number of officials were appointed, each with special responsibilities. The officials in nunneries were, naturally, all women. You can see some of the most important on this page. As medieval women could not be priests, male chaplains visited the nuns' church every day, to hold services. Elderly, quiet priests were chosen for this task. Church leaders feared that nuns would spend too much time gossiping if a talkative young man was appointed. In the same way, monks labouring in the monastery's fields were forbidden to talk to farm-women working nearby.

In Benedictine monasteries, the abbot was elected by the monks, and was then confirmed (approved) by the bishop or the pope. Most abbots ruled wisely, but it was sometimes a difficult task. Abbot Raffredus, of Farfa in Italy, was poisoned by two monks from his monastery when he tried to introduce St Benedict's rule there in 936.

The Cellarer made sure there was food and drink for the nuns, and looked after the stores.

The Hospitaller provided lodgings for pilgrims and other guests who arrived at the nunnery.

The Infirmarian cared for nuns who were ill, and any sick or old people living at the nunnery.

The Almoner gave gifts of charity – money, food or clothes – to beggars outside the gates.

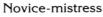

The Novice-mistress taught the girls who were going to be nuns.

Page

Launderer

Messenger

Cook

Groom

Gardener

Builder

Typical monastic servants (left). Monasteries (and nunneries) employed servants to help them prepare food, clean and maintain buildings, go on errands, and run their estates. Servants worked alongside lay-brothers and, sometimes, monks and nuns themselves. Some monasteries were poor, and could not afford many servants; others employed over a hundred.

The chapter house was sometimes used for disciplinary meetings – to investigate laziness or bad behaviour, for example – or to receive special visitors. Bishops made regular tours of inspection, called 'visitations', of all the monasteries in their diocese. They wanted to make sure that monks and nuns were living according to the strict religious rules they had all promised to obey.

LIVING OFF THE LAND

Farming was 'big business' in medieval times. Land equalled wealth. The more land a family – or a monastery – had, the richer it was. After Benedict's reforms, so many people gave land to the Church that vast areas of countryside passed into its control. In 1000, it was estimated that the Church – that is, the Pope, plus dozens of monasteries and nunneries – owned almost a third of Italy.

As we have seen, St Benedict expected that monks would farm this land themselves. It would provide food for the monastery, and give them healthy exercise. They would learn humility and obedience by working like ordinary labourers, doing hard, back-breaking toil. Some monks did work as farmers, and others took on the responsible task of managing their community's estates. But for much of the Middle Ages, lands belonging to monasteries and nunneries were

Decorated initial letters 'E' and 'S' from manuscripts produced by monks working in 11th-century France.

The decorations show monastery servants harvesting grapes (E) and clearing tangled undergrowth (S).

Monks ploughing (above). Monks were allowed to work out of doors like this, but nuns did not have the freedom to leave their nunneries.

More monastic illustrations, from manuscripts probably produced at the monastery of Citeaux in eastern France. These illustrations show: (1) Lay-brothers harvesting corn; (2) Two monks folding a long roll of parchment, to make a book; (3) Lay-brothers chopping wood and clearing land, ready to set up farms near their monastery.

farmed by servants and lay-brothers (men who were part of the monastic community, but had not taken monks' vows), or else by unfree tenants. These were men and women living on the monks' or nuns' land, who had been 'given' to the community by their landlord with the land. They and their descendants could not move elsewhere – they belonged to the monastic estate. Unfree people could not become monks or nuns, according to medieval law. Some estates treated these tenants fairly; others exploited them.

Left
Because monks could read and write, monasteries kept detailed financial records, like this 14th-century rental (list of rent payments) from England.

Once land was given to a monastery, it could not be taken back. The English king Edward I was so alarmed by the wealth and power of the Church that in 1279 he passed a law forbidding landowners to give any more land to monasteries or churches.

FOOD AND DRINK

A monastic 'cartoon' suggesting that the monk chosen to be Cellarer might easily be tempted to drink too much wine.

What is your image of a medieval monk? A fat, red-faced glutton, as seen in films and on TV? Or a thin vegetarian, which is what St Benedict advised? In reality, most monks and nuns were neither one nor the other. They ate reasonable quantities of simple food, thankful that, unlike many other medieval people, they were free from the threat of starvation.

Some monks and nuns did overeat, or develop a taste for luxuries if they got the chance. A few monasteries built enormous kitchens, suggesting that the inhabitants ate very well. In other communities, monks and nuns went to extremes of self-denial, because they believed it would purify their souls. The Church taught that all Christians should fast (go without food, or at least not eat meat) during Lent, on Fridays, and before important festivals.

By modern standards, most monastery meals were plain, and perhaps rather boring. Monks and nuns ate produce from their farms – bread or porridge, cheese, eggs, fresh and dried vegetables, and fruit. They were not meant to eat meat unless they were ill, but this rule was often ignored. Monks and nuns drank weak ale, or wine and water mixed. The alcohol killed germs, but was not strong enough to make the monks drunk.

This circular kitchen, at Fontevrault nunnery in France, was built with an oven at the base of each little tower.

Bread was baked in huge brick ovens. A peel – like a long-handled shovel – was used to take the cooked bread out.

Pigs reared on the monastery farms were fattened in the autumn, then killed and smoked or salted for winter meat.

Monasteries were famous for their gardens, where monks grew all kinds of medicinal herbs, as well as fruit and vegetables for cooking. These gardens (left), at the ancient abbey of Corbie in France, were first described in pictures in the 17th century.

Nuns at a convent in Italy (right) listening to readings from a holy book while they eat.

The magnificent refectory (eating-hall) at Royaumont monastery (below), near Paris, was built with a carved stone pulpit as part of one wall.

The monks' lavatory (left) at Rievaulx Abbey, in northern England.

Lavatories

Novices' room

Cellar

Decorated taps made of brass (above), discovered by archaeologists at monastic sites in England.

Stale urine was used in the making of leather and parchment, and to dye wool. Monks collected it in urinals like this (below), and stored it for future use.

CLEANLINESS

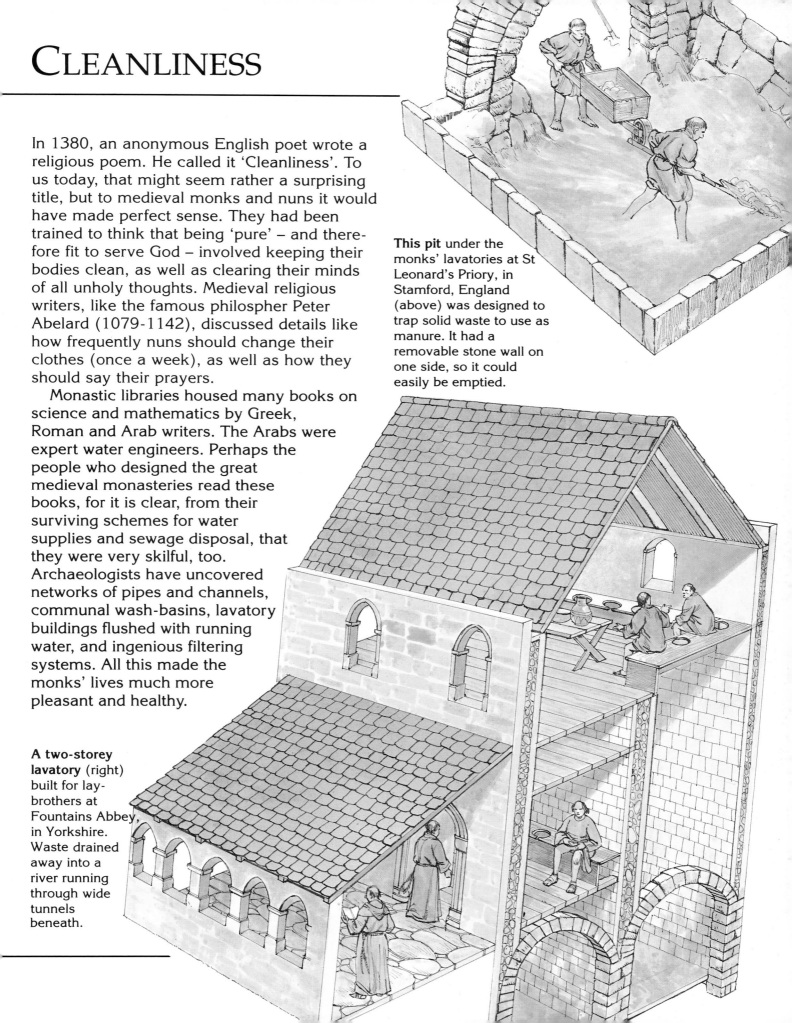

In 1380, an anonymous English poet wrote a religious poem. He called it 'Cleanliness'. To us today, that might seem rather a surprising title, but to medieval monks and nuns it would have made perfect sense. They had been trained to think that being 'pure' – and therefore fit to serve God – involved keeping their bodies clean, as well as clearing their minds of all unholy thoughts. Medieval religious writers, like the famous philospher Peter Abelard (1079-1142), discussed details like how frequently nuns should change their clothes (once a week), as well as how they should say their prayers.

Monastic libraries housed many books on science and mathematics by Greek, Roman and Arab writers. The Arabs were expert water engineers. Perhaps the people who designed the great medieval monasteries read these books, for it is clear, from their surviving schemes for water supplies and sewage disposal, that they were very skilful, too. Archaeologists have uncovered networks of pipes and channels, communal wash-basins, lavatory buildings flushed with running water, and ingenious filtering systems. All this made the monks' lives much more pleasant and healthy.

This pit under the monks' lavatories at St Leonard's Priory, in Stamford, England (above) was designed to trap solid waste to use as manure. It had a removable stone wall on one side, so it could easily be emptied.

A two-storey lavatory (right) built for lay-brothers at Fountains Abbey, in Yorkshire. Waste drained away into a river running through wide tunnels beneath.

LOVE THY NEIGHBOUR

Jesus told his followers to care for other people, not just to look after themselves. How could monks and nuns put these teachings into practice? One way was to set up hospitals, to care for sick and homeless people, travellers, and orphans. By the 14th century, there were over 700 in England alone. The biggest were built in cities, where people lived crowded together in unhealthy conditions.

Medieval hospitals were staffed by nuns, helped by lay-sisters and female servants. Unlike other nunneries, you did not have to be rich or noble to join. The work was hard and dirty, and there was always the risk of infection. Most hospitals had primitive sanitation and no running water.

Nuns receiving patients at the great medieval hospital, the Hotel-Dieu in Paris, France. Run by nuns, lay-sisters and servants, this hospital treated all illnesses except leprosy. By the late 15th century, the staff cared for between 400-500 patients at any one time. Tasks included washing and feeding patients, making and giving medicines, and arranging burials.

Abdominal surgery (above), as shown in a medieval medical manuscript. The patient was drugged with alcohol and herbs to lessen the pain.

Nuns hang sheets to dry from an upstairs balcony at the Hotel-Dieu (below). Running a hospital involved vast amounts of laundry. Without modern machines to help, it all had to be done by hand.

Woman with leprosy (above).

Medieval treatments (right):
1. Fixing a splint.
2. Examining a sprain.
3, 4. Treating a dislocated shoulder.
5. Comforting a patient.
6. Blood-letting.

Nuns also nursed people with leprosy, blind people, mothers and babies, and old people . Nuns living as anchorites (like hermits, but in towns), listened to people's problems and gave advice.

Only men could train as doctors; their fees were expensive, and their treatments were uncertain and sometimes alarming. Women acted as carers, and as 'unoffical' healers. There were some male nurses, and also soldier-monks called Knights Hospitallers, who originally treated Crusaders fighting in the Holy Land.

Medical students at a lecture (above). Monastic libraries contained many books on medicine, herbs and healing.

REFORMERS

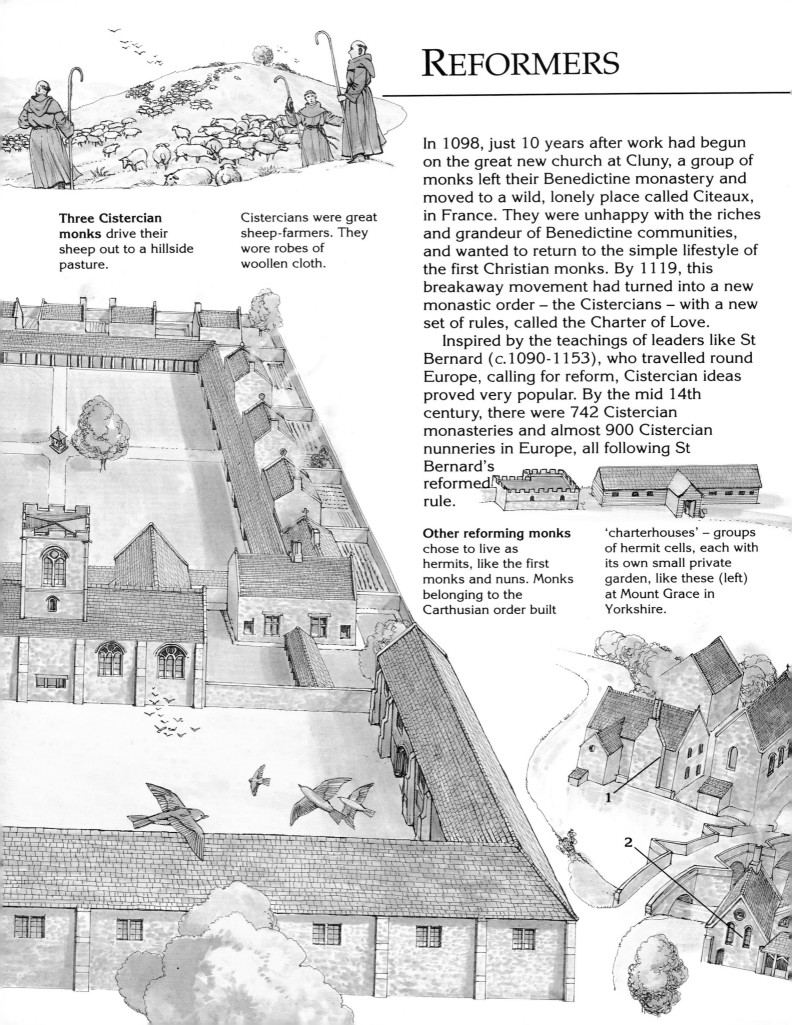

Three Cistercian monks drive their sheep out to a hillside pasture.

Cistercians were great sheep-farmers. They wore robes of woollen cloth.

In 1098, just 10 years after work had begun on the great new church at Cluny, a group of monks left their Benedictine monastery and moved to a wild, lonely place called Citeaux, in France. They were unhappy with the riches and grandeur of Benedictine communities, and wanted to return to the simple lifestyle of the first Christian monks. By 1119, this breakaway movement had turned into a new monastic order – the Cistercians – with a new set of rules, called the Charter of Love.

Inspired by the teachings of leaders like St Bernard (c.1090-1153), who travelled round Europe, calling for reform, Cistercian ideas proved very popular. By the mid 14th century, there were 742 Cistercian monasteries and almost 900 Cistercian nunneries in Europe, all following St Bernard's reformed rule.

Other reforming monks chose to live as hermits, like the first monks and nuns. Monks belonging to the Carthusian order built 'charterhouses' – groups of hermit cells, each with its own small private garden, like these (left) at Mount Grace in Yorkshire.

St Bernard said that Cistercian monks and nuns should live in remote places, away from the busy world. They should spend much less time in church, and much more time at work. Their buildings should be plain and undecorated, and their services should be simple, but uplifting.

These were noble aims, but they were not fulfilled. Because people admired the Cistercians, they gave them land. But the monks and nuns had so much time to devote to farming that they soon became rich. By 1191, Cistercian leaders themselves admitted that 'love of property has become a scourge.'

Fountains Abbey (below) in North Yorkshire:
1. Guesthouses.
2. Lay brothers' infirmary.
3. Lay brothers' dormitory and refectory.
4. Kitchen.
5. Monks' refectory.
6. Warming room.
7. Cloister.
8. Abbey church.
9. Chapter house.
10. Monks' dormitory.
11. Abbot's house.
12. Infirmary.
13. Infirmary lavatory.
14. Cemetery.

There were also gardens, barns, a bakehouse, a malthouse, stables and a gatehouse (not shown here).

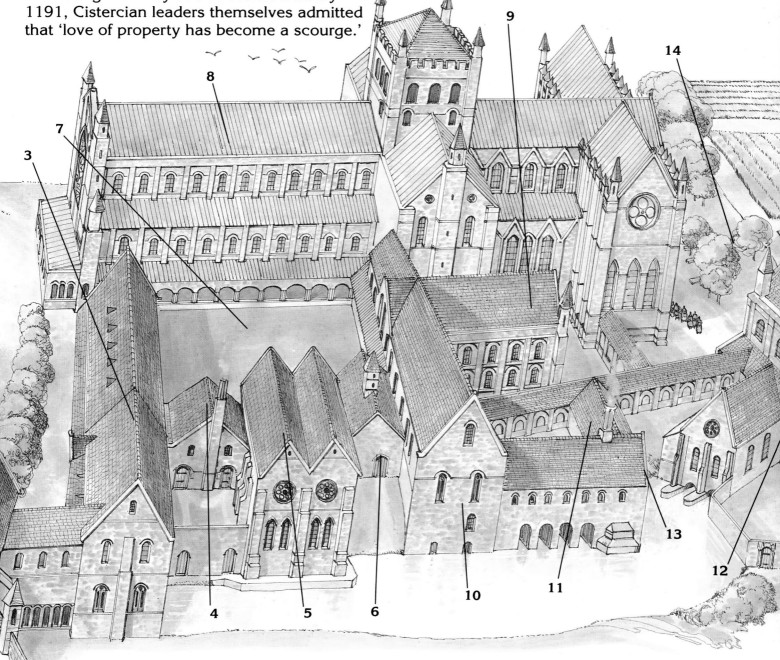

FRIARS AND PILGRIMS

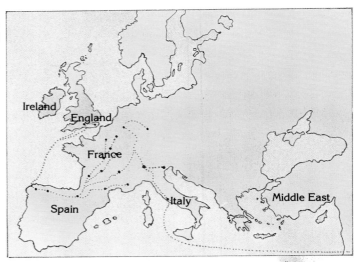

St Bernard was not the only medieval churchman to criticise the Benedictine rule. By the 13th century, some people were going further, and asking whether monks and nuns were really needed at all. Two remarkable men, St Francis (1182-1226) and St Dominic (1170-1221), thought not. To replace them, they set up orders of friars ('brothers'), who lived among ordinary men and women, preaching and teaching the Christian faith. Friars attracted crowds wherever they went; by the 15th century, many large churches had been built (by generous patrons), to house the vast congregations who came to listen to their sermons.

For centuries, monks and nuns had been Christian 'pioneers'. Their communities had served as Christian strongholds in an often hostile world. But, after around 1200, things were beginning to change. Ordinary people started to play a more active role in religion. They gave money to build great cathedrals and local parish churches; they went on pilgrimages – journeys with a religious purpose; and they set up religious guilds (charity clubs). Monasteries and nunneries were no longer the only places of learning; new schools and universities were founded, where men who were neither monks nor priests could live, study and teach.

Pilgrim routes across Europe (above). Pilgrims travelled long distances and faced hardship and danger to travel to the shrine of a favourite saint. Legends grew up, telling how certain saints had performed healing miracles or brought astonishing good luck in return for prayers.

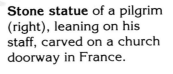

Stone statue of a pilgrim (right), leaning on his staff, carved on a church doorway in France.

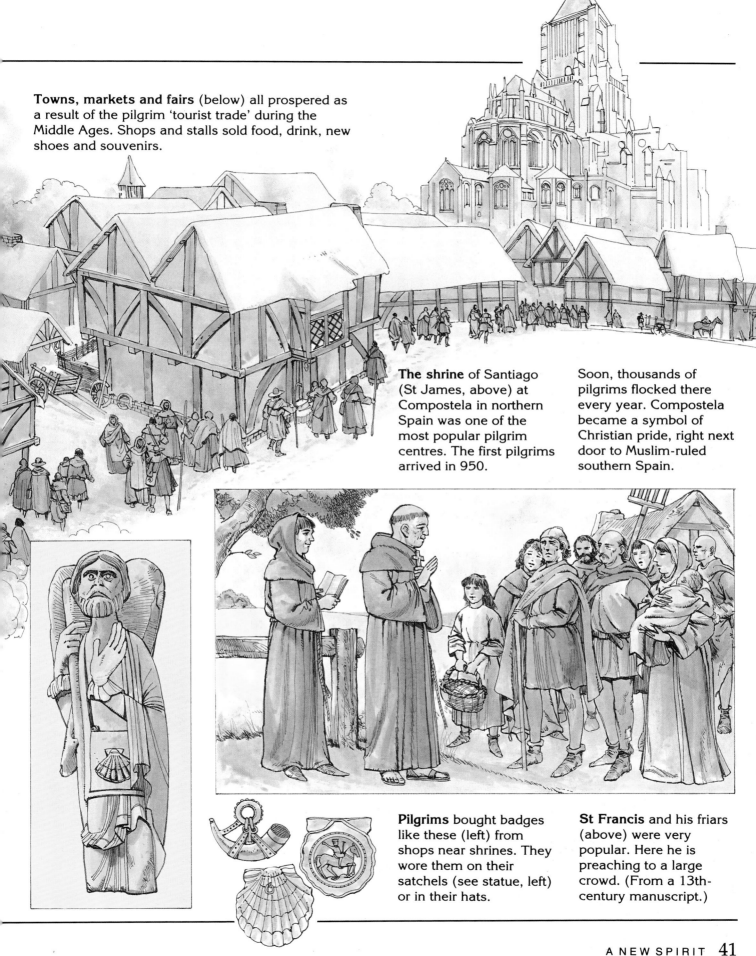

Towns, markets and fairs (below) all prospered as a result of the pilgrim 'tourist trade' during the Middle Ages. Shops and stalls sold food, drink, new shoes and souvenirs.

The shrine of Santiago (St James, above) at Compostela in northern Spain was one of the most popular pilgrim centres. The first pilgrims arrived in 950.

Soon, thousands of pilgrims flocked there every year. Compostela became a symbol of Christian pride, right next door to Muslim-ruled southern Spain.

Pilgrims bought badges like these (left) from shops near shrines. They wore them on their satchels (see statue, left) or in their hats.

St Francis and his friars (above) were very popular. Here he is preaching to a large crowd. (From a 13th-century manuscript.)

MONASTERIES AROUND THE WORLD

This book has described Christian monasteries and nunneries in medieval Europe. But religious communities like this have existed – and still exist – in many different parts of the world. Not all monasteries are Christian. Members of other faiths, especially Buddhism and Taoism (both popular in the Far East), have lived together in religious communities.

European monasteries and nunneries have often been criticised. One 12th century priest called them 'prisons of the damned'. In his *Canterbury Tales*, the English poet Geoffrey Chaucer (1343-1400) described a vain, silly Prioress, who cared only for elegant clothes and her pets. In the early 16th century, a bishop visiting monks at Wymondham in Norfolk discovered that their library contained only cookery books, not books

8th-century cave-dwellings (left) carved from the rock by monks in the Goreme Valley, in Turkey.

The monastery of Rila, Bulgaria (above). Founded in the 10th century and rebuilt many times.

Zagorsk monastery (below), near Moscow, contains 6 churches, a bishop's palace and pilgrim hostels.

Grande Chartreuse monastery (above), founded in the 12th century in a remote valley in the French Alps.

The 8th-century monastery of Reichenau, south Germany, built, for safety, on an island in a lake. It soon became famous as a centre of learning, attracting scholars from as far away as Ireland and Northumbria.

about religion. Religious communities have also been attacked for political reasons. In 17th century Germany, monks and nuns were massacred in bloody civil wars. In 1789, the French revolutionary government 'nationalised' all Church property, to raise money for the state. In the 1960s, Buddhist monasteries in Tibet were destroyed, because they opposed Mao Zhedong's government in Beijing.

However, in spite of all these difficulties, monasteries and nunneries have survived. Now, as in the past, some are good and some are bad. But many still offer a peaceful refuge, a centre of learning, or a source of community service to millions of people.

Throughout the world, people of different faiths have built beautiful monasteries, where monks can devote their lives to prayer. Many are still in use today. This Buddhist monastery (below, left) is in Bangkok, the capital city of Thailand.

By 1540, King Henry VIII of England had closed down all English monasteries and ordered their lands and buildings to be sold. Most are now in ruins, like Lindisfarne monastery (below), off the Northumbrian coast of England.

THE MEDIEVAL CHURCH

The medieval Church was a large, wealthy, complicated organisation, staffed by men with many different ranks and tasks. There were very few 'official' jobs for women, but they still played an important part in medieval religious life. Over the centuries, the Church changed. Some of the earliest Church bodies, such as monasteries, were replaced by new, more dynamic groups. These pages will give you an 'overview' of the medieval Church and the men and women who worked for it from around AD 400–1500.

PRIESTS

Priests were the basic 'building blocks' of the Church structure. All of Europe was divided into parishes, small areas of land about the same size as an average village. Each parish needed a priest, to say services in the parish church (or in the open air, if there wasn't one), and to guide and teach the parishioners about the Christian faith.

It took several years to become a priest. First, a man took 'minor orders'; that is, he promised to serve God, live a good life, and obey Church officials. He was then given a series of minor jobs, all based at the parish church. First of all he was door-keeper, then 'lector' (he helped read and sing the church services), then 'exorcist' – he said prayers to remove evil spirits. Finally he became an 'acolyte', permitted to help the priests with the most sacred moments of church services.

The next step was to be 'ordained' (appointed and blessed) to the rank of deacon. Deacons could perform almost all the tasks – in church and out in the parish, helping parishioners – that a priest could do, except take the Mass.

When their training was complete, priests were appointed to care for a parish. After the 12th century, neither priests nor deacons could marry. Only priests were eligible for the top jobs in the Church administration.

MONKS AND NUNS

In this book, we have seen how the monastic lifestyle developed from groups of individual men and women, who had chosen to live a solitary life as hermits, joining together for help, support and safety.

The first monks worked out their own rules for living. These varied from place to place. Major differences developed between the Celtic church – in Ireland, Scotland, northern England and parts of France – and the rest of Christian Europe, which followed instructions received from Rome. Celtic and Roman monasteries were also different. Celtic communities were often built to house monks and nuns, living in separate buildings but working and worshipping together. Some Celtic 'double' monasteries were headed by women, like the wise and learned St Hilda of Whitby (died 680). Problems caused by the two different Christian 'systems' were finally solved at the Synod of Whitby in 664.

After around 950, the majority of monks and nuns in Europe followed the Benedictine Rule, which is described in detail on pages 14/15 of this book. It gradually became less popular, as new monastic leaders, from the 12th century onwards, called for reform.

Novice-mistress

REFORMERS

During the Middle Ages, reforming monks and nuns found many reasons to criticise monasteries and nunneries. This was probably not surprising: it is extremely difficult for any organisation – like a religious community – which demands a strict, disciplined, self-denying lifestyle from its members to keep to its original high ideals and noble aims. Here are some of the most important reform movements:

Carthusians (men)
A very strict hermit order, founded by St Bruno of Cologne (Germany) in 1084. He felt that existing monasteries were too much like ordinary, comfortable noble homes. Carthusians lived in individual cells, and met only in church. Apart from hymns and prayers, they kept complete silence at all times. Many worked as craftsmen.

Cistercian monks and nuns
(men and women)
St Bernard of Clairvaux 1090–1153 preached against extravagance and luxury, particularly in monastic buildings. He wanted monks and nuns to live pure, simple lives. He helped to establish a new 'family' (an 'order') of monasteries and nunneries, called the Cistercians. Cistercian monks and nuns built communities in wild, lonely places, and spent more time working, and less time praying, than Benedictines did.

Franciscan and Dominican Friars
(men, all priests)
Founded during the 13th century, as an alternative to the old monastic communities. The friars aimed to travel the world, preaching and teaching. They became extremely popular, and attracted large crowds. You can read more about the friars on pages 40/41.

Augustinian Canons and Canonesses
Groups of people, attached to cathedral churches, who lived in communities known as 'colleges'. Re-organised in 1059, they lived according to a rule originally drawn up by the 4th-century bishop St Augustine. Many were famous scholars.

Premonstratensian Canons and Canonesses
Founded in 1120. They also lived in colleges, usually in towns, did social work and were missionaries.

OTHER GROUPS
Beghards (men) and *Beguines* (women)
Groups of ordinary men and women who lived in communities dedicated to God, but not shut away from the world like monks and nuns. Flourished in the 14th and 15th centuries. They did teaching and social work, and also provided an environment where people who did not have the money needed to enter a monastic community could still live a religious life.

Hermits, Anchorites (men and women)
People who lived alone, without complicated monastic rules to guide them. They spent most of their time in religious study or in prayer. Sometimes their cells were built next to parish churches, so they could share in community worship. Sometimes they offered spiritual counselling or guidance; sometimes they were mystics. Famous mystical anchorites included Christina of Markyate (12th century) and Julian of Norwich (14th century).

Knight Templar

Knights Hospitaller and Knights Templar (men)
These were two orders of warrior monks, formed in the 11th century to fight alongside Crusaders in the holy land. They also had special duties; Hospitallers cared for the sick. Templars looked after holy shrines in Jerusalem.

GLOSSARY

Almoner, monk in charge of giving charity to the poor.

Altar, a special table in a church, where Mass was celebrated. It was often decorated with paintings, crosses, gold and jewels.

Apostles, men who had known Jesus, and who had been chosen by him to spread the new faith.

Archangel, high-ranking angel. Medieval people believed that angels were messengers from God.

Archbishop, a senior church leader, responsible for administering a wide area, called a province.

Benedictines, monks and nuns who followed the rule of St Benedict (c AD 480-550).

Bishop, a church leader, in charge of a diocese.

Cellarer, person in charge of food stores.

Cells, little rooms.

Celtic, the lands where the ancient Celtic peoples lived. In the Middle Ages, used to describe Scotland, Ireland, Wales, Cornwall and Brittany, in France.

Chaplain, a priest who works as a religious advisor to a family or an organisation.

Chapter House, meeting room in a monastery or nunnery.

Chastity, living a pure life, without sex.

Cistercians, monks and nuns who followed the reformed rule drawn up at the monastery of Citeaux, France.

Cloisters, the courtyard next to a monastic church, with a surrounding covered walkway, where monks or nuns could walk or sit, read and study.

Cluniac, monks who copied the rich lifestyle of the Benedictine monastery at Cluny, France.

Community, in this book, another word for a monastery or a nunnery.

Congregation, a group of worshippers in church.

Crucified, nailed to a cross and left to die. A cruel way of executing criminals, used in Roman times.

Deacon, a trainee priest. Men who wanted a career in the church first took minor orders, then became deacons, and finally were ordained as priests. Very capable (or very holy) priests might eventually become bishops or archbishops.

Diocese, a division within the administrative structure of the Church, ruled by a bishop. An area the size of several English counties.

Dislocated, pushed out of place.

Eternal, everlasting.

Fast, to go without food or water, or to give up foods that you enjoy. Medieval Christians fasted to show God they were sorry for their sins.

Friars ('brothers'), travelling priests who devoted their lives to preaching. There were two main groups (called orders) of friars, the Franciscans (or Greyfriars), founded by St Francis of Assisi, and the Dominicans (or Blackfriars) founded by St Dominic.

Hermit, someone who lives alone, to be able to concentrate entirely on God.

Holy Spirit, Christians believe that God's Holy Spirit – a powerful force for good – is still at work in the world today. In the Middle Ages, people prayed to the Holy Spirit to ask for help.

Infirmarian, monk or nun in charge of the community's hospital.

Lay-brothers, men who lived and worked in a monastery, but did not take full vows as monks. There were lay-sisters in some nunneries, too.

Mass, the most holy service held by the Church, when specially blessed bread and wine – believed also to be Jesus's body and blood – are shared among the priests and people in church. (In medieval times, only priests sipped the wine.) Christians believe that Jesus is with them at each Mass.

Missionary, someone who teaches a new religion.

Monastic, to do with monks or monasteries. In this book, refers to nuns and nunneries as well.

Mortar, a sticky mixture (sand, lime and water) that is used to hold building stones together.

Novices, people training to become monks or nuns.

Parchment, specially prepared sheepskin or goatskin, used for writing.

Patrons, wealthy, powerful men and women who gave money to monasteries and nunneries.

Pilgrimage, visit to a sacred shrine. Some pilgrimages were deeply religious, others were more like a holiday.

Plain-song, a type of singing, popular in monasteries and nunneries.

Priest, someone employed by the Church to hold services and look after the men and women living in a particular parish. Priests had to be ordained (specially blessed) by a bishop, before they could do these tasks. In the Middle Ages, only healthy adult men could be priests.

Prophet, someone who believes they have a message from God to share with the world.

Quill, a pen made from a goose wing-feather.

Reliquary, a beautiful container, made to hold the relics of a saint.

Saint, someone who has lived an especially good and holy life.

Shrine, the place where relics were displayed.

Silver-gilt, silver covered with a very thin layer of gold.

Stylus, a long, strong pin, used for writing.

Tracery, cut-out patterns.

Tonsure, a special haircut, worn by monks. It was copied from the ancient Roman habit of shaving the heads of slaves, to show their low status. Monks were God's slaves, so their hair was also (partly) removed. Women had their hair cut short when they became nuns.

Vow, a promise. Monks and nuns promised 'Poverty, Chastity and Obedience'.

INDEX